Scripture quoted from the
International Children's Bible,
New Century Version. Used by permission.

This edition published by Family Christian Press
5300 Patterson Avenue SE, Grand Rapids, MI 49530
Produced by RD Publishing Services
Reader's Digest Road, Pleasantville, NY 10570-7000
Printed in China
10 9 8 7 6 5 4 3 2 1

# The Newborn King

Written by Gaylyn Williams
Illustrated by Allan Eitzen

FAMILY
CHRISTIAN
PRESS

# Isaiah prophesies about Jesus.

Long before Jesus was born, God talked to a man named Isaiah. God told Isaiah, "I am going to send a baby to earth. This baby will be my own son, Jesus. He will save everyone in the world from their sins." Then Isaiah told the people what God said.

*A prayer to pray:*
*Thank you, God, that long ago,*
*even before Isaiah lived,*
*you planned to send Jesus to earth*
*to give us a new start.*

**A verse to memorize:**
"God loved the world so much that he gave his only son" (John 3:16).

# An angel talks to Mary.

Mary and Joseph were going to get married soon. One day an angel appeared to Mary. Mary was scared of the angel, but the angel said, "You don't need to be afraid. God is going to do a miracle. You will have a baby. That baby will be God's own son. He will save all of us from our sins."

Mary and the angel talked, and the angel answered Mary's questions. Soon Mary wasn't afraid. She was happy to do what God wanted.

### A prayer to pray:
*Lord, Mary asked you questions.*
*I'm glad I can ask you questions, too.*
*And I know you can answer them,*
*because nothing is too hard for you.*

### A verse to memorize:
"God can do everything" (Luke 1:37).

# The trip to Bethlehem.

Mary would soon have the baby. The king said, "Go to Bethlehem to be counted." So Mary and Joseph rode on donkeys for many days to get to Bethlehem. It was a hard trip.

"I'm so tired," said Mary. "I think it's almost time for my baby to come."

"We're almost there," Joseph said. "Look, I can see Bethlehem now."

### A song to sing:
*"O little town of Bethlehem, how still we see thee lie!*
*Above thy deep and dreamless sleep the silent stars go by.*
*Yet in thy dark streets shineth the everlasting light;*
*The hopes and fears of all the years are met in thee tonight."*

**question to answer:**
ow long do you think it took for Mary and Joseph to reach Bethlehem?

# Finding the stable.

When Mary and Joseph got to Bethlehem, they were very tired. But when they tried to find a place to stay, every innkeeper said, "I'm sorry—no room." All the inns were full.

Finally, a kind man said, "You can stay in my stable with the animals, if you want." So Mary and Joseph slept on the straw with the sheep and cows.

### A prayer to pray:
*Dear Lord, thank you for giving me
a nice house and a soft bed
where I can sleep.
I'm glad I don't have to sleep on
straw in a stable with sheep and cows.
I'm happy I have a place to stay.*

## Questions to answer:

Where were you born? How is it different from where Jesus was born?

# Jesus is born.

"Joseph, the baby is coming," Mary said.
That night the baby was born in the stable.
Only the animals were there with them.

"We'll call him Jesus," said Joseph, "just like
the angel told us."

Mary wrapped Jesus in soft cloths and
lovingly laid him in a box where the animals ate.

*A song to sing:*
*"Away in a manger, no crib for a bed,*
*The little Lord Jesus laid down his sweet head;*
*The stars in the sky looked down where he lay,*
*The little Lord Jesus, asleep on the hay."*

## Questions to answer:

How many animals do you see? Can you name
the kinds of animals?

# Angels appear to the shepherds.

On the hills near the town of Bethlehem, shepherds watched their sheep. The night was dark and cold, so the shepherds huddled around a fire. Everything was very, very still.

Suddenly, a bright light lit up the sky. An angel appeared! The shepherds were scared. But the angel said, "Don't be afraid. I have good news! Tonight the Savior has been born. You'll find him in a manger in Bethlehem." Then many angels appeared and sang praises to God.

*A prayer to pray:*
*Dear Lord Jesus, thank you for*
*the good news the angel brought.*
*Thank you for helping*
*the shepherds not to be afraid.*
*Thank you for coming*
*to fill my heart with joy, not fear.*

**A verse to memorize:**
"Give glory to God in heaven" (Luke 2:14).

# The shepherds find Jesus.

After the angels left, one shepherd shouted, "Let's go find this baby. He's our Savior." So the shepherds ran to find baby Jesus. They found him lying in a manger.

When the shepherds left the stable, they told everyone they met about Jesus. They praised God, because everything happened just like the angel said.

**A prayer to pray:**
Dear God, please help me to be bold like the
shepherds and tell other people about Jesus.

**A song to sing:**
"O come let us adore him, O come let us adore him,
O come let us adore him, Christ the Lord.
For he alone is worthy, For he alone is worthy,
For he alone is worthy, Christ the Lord."

**W**ise men bring presents to the newborn king.

For many days wise men had followed a star from a country that was far away. "Look, the star stopped over Bethlehem," a wise man said.

"Let's go see this newborn king," urged another wise man.

When they saw Jesus, they knelt down and worshiped him. Then they gave him their best gifts. The wise men were so happy God led them to see the new king.

### Something to do:

What gift can you give to Jesus?